Wet, Blue, and Good for You

by Ellen Lawrence

Consultant:

Judy Wearing, PhD, BEd
Faculty of Education, Queen's University
Ontario, Canada

BEARPORT
PUBLISHING

New York, New York

Credits

Cover, © Maxim Blinkov/Shutterstock; 4, © Fotokostic/Shutterstock; 5, © Jorg Hackemann/Shutterstock; 6, © Larisa Lofitskaya/Shutterstock; 7, © DoublePHOTO studio/Shutterstock; 7R, © Science Photo Library; 8L, © mylisa/Shutterstock; 8R, © dr OX/Shutterstock; 9, © adike/Shutterstock; 10T, © Antonio Guillem/Shutterstock; 10B, © RomanenkoAlexey/Shutterstock; 11, © sabza/Shutterstock; 12, © Osokina Liudmila/Shutterstock; 13, © leungchopan/Shutterstock, © Samuel Borges Photography/Shutterstock, and © sciencepics/Shutterstock; 14, © Artit Thongchuea/Shutterstock; 15, © August_0802/Shutterstock; 16, © czuber/Depositphotos; 17, © ChiccoDodiFC/Shutterstock; 18T, © Cheryl Casey/Dreamstime; 18B, © Kamira/Shutterstock; 19, © Jaimie Duplass/Shutterstock; 20T, © Darrin Henry/Shutterstock; 20B, © Chatchai Somwat/Shutterstock; 21, © Africa Studio/Shutterstock; 22, © liza54500/Shutterstock, © ben bryant/Shutterstock, © Silverfoxz/Shutterstock, © Olga Kovalenko/Shutterstock, and © Yuriy Boyko/Shutterstock; 23TL, © Science Photo Library; 23TC, © Maridav/Shutterstock; 23TR, © Maridav/Shutterstock; 23BL, © sciencepics/Shutterstock; 23BC, © Larisa Lofitskaya/Shutterstock; 23BR, © g-stockstudio/Shutterstock.

Publisher: Kenn Goin
Editor: Jessica Rudolph
Creative Director: Spencer Brinker
Design: Emma Randall
Photo Researcher: Ruby Tuesday Books Ltd

Library of Congress Cataloging-in-Publication Data

Names: Lawrence, Ellen, 1967– author.
Title: Wet, blue, and good for you / by Ellen Lawrence.
Description: New York, New York : Bearport Publishing, [2016] | Series: Drip,
   drip, drop: Earth's water | Audience: Ages 6–10. | Includes
   bibliographical references and index.
Identifiers: LCCN 2015040327 (print) | LCCN 2015041639 (ebook) | ISBN
   9781943553259 (library binding) | ISBN 9781943553594 (ebook)
Subjects: LCSH: Water—Physiological effect—Juvenile literature. |
   Dehydration (Physiology)—Juvenile literature.
Classification: LCC QP535.HI L39 2016 (print) | LCC QP535.HI (ebook) | DDC
   613—dc23
LC record available at http://lccn.loc.gov/2015040327

For more information, write to Bearport Publishing Company, Inc., 45 West 21st Street, Suite 3B, New York, New York 10010. Printed in the United States of America.

10 9 8 7 6 5 4 3 2 1

Contents

Feeling Thirsty

If you play soccer on a hot day, you may start to feel thirsty.

This is your body's way of telling you it needs water.

You take a drink and the thirsty feeling goes away.

So why does your body need water, and where does it go once you swallow it?

Without water, your body cannot work properly. In fact, a person can only survive for a few days with no water!

5

We're All Made of Water

Every part of your body—even your blood—is made up of billions of tiny **cells**.

To keep your body working, your cells need things like **oxygen** and **nutrients**.

These substances travel through your blood, which is mostly made of water!

Your body takes in nutrients when you eat and drink.

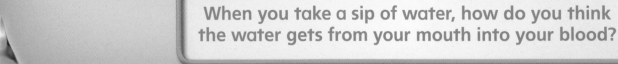

When you take a sip of water, how do you think the water gets from your mouth into your blood?

6

This photo was taken by a powerful microscope.

skin cells

Your skin, bones, and every other part of your body are made of cells. All cells contain water. In fact, your body is about 60 percent water!

Water for Making Blood

When you drink water, it goes from your mouth to your stomach.

Then the water travels to your intestines, where it's released into your blood.

Blood is made up of red and white blood cells and a liquid called plasma.

Plasma, a very important ingredient, is mostly made of water.

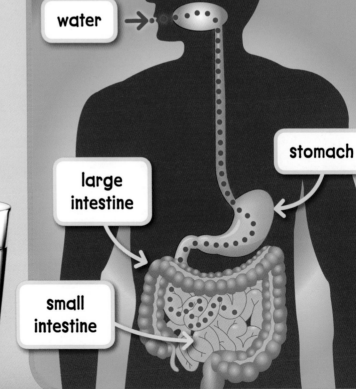

water

stomach

large intestine

small intestine

The Main Ingredients in Blood

It's the watery plasma that makes your blood runny.

Blood flows through your body in billions of tiny tubes.

Red blood cells give blood its color.

White blood cells help our bodies fight germs.

Your Blood in Action

As blood flows around your body, plasma delivers water and nutrients to your cells.

When blood passes through your lungs, red blood cells pick up oxygen.

Then the oxygen is delivered to other cells throughout your body.

Without water, your body wouldn't have the blood needed to do all this important work!

You breathe oxygen into your lungs.

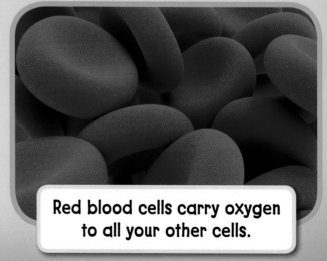

Red blood cells carry oxygen to all your other cells.

Nutrients get into your blood the same way water does. When you eat, food travels to the stomach and then to the small intestine. The small intestine soaks up nutrients from the food and releases them into your blood.

Nutrients in food give your cells energy.

Your body also uses water to make a liquid that helps you eat. What do you think this liquid is?
(The answer is on page 24.)

11

Removing Waste

The water you drink also helps keep your body clean on the inside. How?

As cells use oxygen and nutrients, they create unwanted gases and **chemicals**.

This waste is carried away from your cells by your blood.

Then the blood takes the waste to your **kidneys**.

Your blood flows through your two kidneys about 400 times each day.

kidneys

After the cells' waste is taken to your kidneys, water helps carry the waste out of your body. How do you think this happens?

13

Water Goes In and Water Goes Out

What do kidneys do with waste?

They get rid of it!

The kidneys turn any water your body doesn't need into urine, or pee.

Then, when you go to the bathroom, the pee leaves your body and carries waste along with it.

When you don't drink enough water, your kidneys try to stop too much water from leaving your body. They only make a small amount of urine—just enough to remove waste from your body.

Sometimes pee is very pale yellow. At other times, it can be dark yellow. Why do you think this is? (The answer is on page 24.)

Cooling Off

The water you drink also helps your body stay cool.

When you get too hot, your skin makes sweat.

Sweat contains some chemicals from inside the body, but it's mostly made of water.

This liquid cools off your skin.

As it dries, sweat also draws out some of the heat from your body.

sweat

An adult who exercises can produce several pints of sweat in a day. About half a pint (0.24 l) of this sweat is released through the feet.

Not Enough Water

If you don't drink enough water, you can become **dehydrated**.

For example, this may happen if you sweat a lot when exercising.

You might feel dizzy, get a headache, or have trouble concentrating.

A very dehydrated person may even get seriously ill and have to go to the hospital.

Being dehydrated can sometimes make you feel like you need something to eat. Drinking water may make the hungry feeling go away.

19

Wet, Blue, and Good for You

To be healthy and have lots of energy, your body needs water.

Drinking water will help you concentrate on your schoolwork and feel less tired.

So make sure you drink plenty of water every day.

Never ignore that thirsty feeling—it's your body telling you it needs a drink!

Why do you think it's important to drink water when you're playing sports?
(The answer is on page 24.)

You can get some water by eating fruits and vegetables. Apples and carrots are about 85 percent water. Cucumbers and tomatoes are more than 90 percent water!

When you eat a juicy orange, you get nutrients and water. Yet how much of an orange is water? Let's investigate!

How Much Water Is in an Orange?

1. Weigh the orange and record the weight in a notebook.

What do you think the orange will weigh after all its juice has been removed?

Write your prediction in your notebook.

2. Ask an adult to help you cut the orange into several thin slices.

3. Place a sheet of foil on a flat surface in a warm place, such as a sunny windowsill. Put the paper towel on top of the foil. Then lay the orange slices on the paper towel.

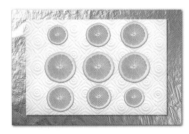

4. Allow the slices to get dry and crispy. This may take two or three days.

5. Once the orange slices are dry, weigh them all at once.

How much does the orange weigh now? What's the difference between the orange's weight before and after it was dried? Does this match your prediction?

(The answers are on page 24.)

Science Words

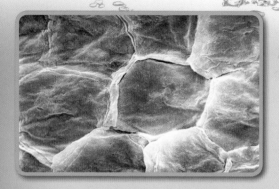

cells (SELZ) very tiny parts of a person, animal, or plant; cells are too small to see with our eyes alone

chemicals (KEM-uh-kuhlz) natural or human-made substances; our bodies remove waste chemicals in our urine

dehydrated (dee-HYE-dray-tid) not having enough water in a person's body

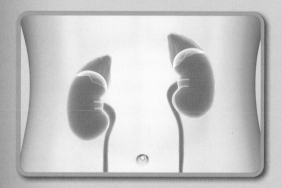

kidneys (KID-neez) the pair of body parts that remove waste from the blood and turn water and waste into urine

nutrients (NOO-tree-uhnts) substances, such as vitamins and protein, that a person needs to grow, get energy, and be healthy

oxygen (OK-suh-juhn) a colorless gas found in air and water, which people and animals need to breathe

Index

Read More

Hewitt, Sally. *Water (Good For Me).* New York: Rosen (2008).

Oxlade, Chris. *Water (How Does My Home Work?).* Mankato, MN: Heinemann-Raintree (2013).

Schuh, Mari C. *Drinking Water (Healthy Eating with MyPyramid).* Mankato, MN: Capstone (2006).

Learn More Online

To learn more about water and your body, visit **www.bearportpublishing.com/DripDripDrop**

About the Author

Ellen Lawrence lives in the United Kingdom. Her favorite books to write are those about nature and animals. In fact, the first book Ellen bought for herself, when she was six years old, was the story of a gorilla named Patty Cake that was born in New York's Central Park Zoo.

Answers

Page 11: Your mouth produces saliva, or spit, which is mostly made of water. This slimy liquid helps your teeth and tongue make your food mushy so it's easy to swallow.

Page 15: When pee contains plenty of water, the color is pale, not dark. When pee is dark yellow, it's usually because it contains less water.

Page 20: When you play sports, your body gets hot and starts to sweat. This means your body is losing water. Therefore, it's important to get a drink of water.

Page 22: Exact weights will vary, but the orange will weigh a lot less after it dries out. This shows that most of an orange's weight is from water.